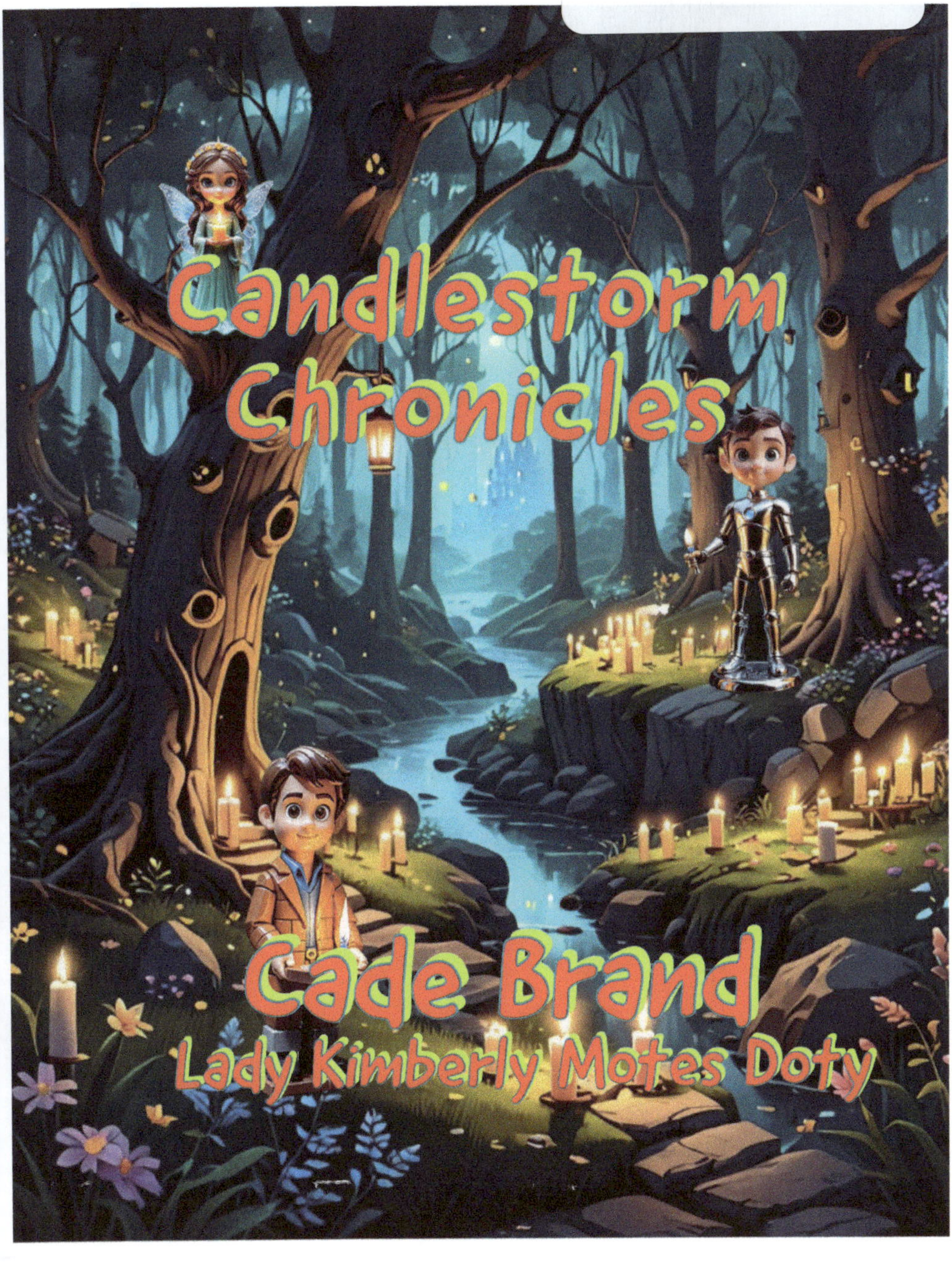

Candlestorm Chronicles

Cade Brand
Lady Kimberly Motes Doty

Candlestorm Chronicles

Cade Brand

Lady Kimberly Motes Doty

ISBN   979-8-3302-1018-3 (paperback book) Ingram

ISBN   979-8-3302-1019-0 (digital ebook) Ingram

ISBN   979-8-3341-6635-6 (paperback book) Amazon

ASIN   B0D8Z3L7DW (digital ebook) Amazon

ISBN   (hardcover book)

ISBN   (audio book)

Lady Kimberly Industries LLC

15019 Madeira Way, #86174

Madeira Beach, Florida 33708-9998

www.LadyKimberlyIndustries.com

https://mybook.to/LadyKimberlyBooks

Cade Brand & Lady Kimberly Motes Doty

Candlestorm Chronicles

By

Cade Brand
&
Lady Kimberly Motes Doty

Once upon a time, in a land where the wind howled fiercely, there lived three little candles in the forest candle village.

These candles were not ordinary;

they had a spark of curiosity,

a flicker of adventure,

and a touch of wisdom.

They would gather together each day, their flames dancing in excitement, wondering what they should do.

"There has to be something we can do if the big bad wind comes back" said the glistening metal candle boy.

"Yes, we have to be able to protect ourselves and our candle forest village" agreed the littlest princess candle.

Just then, the big bad wind arrived.

It was howling and blowing leaves and sticks everywhere through the candle forest village.

It swept through the candle forest village, extinguishing their flames.

The three little candles huddled together, shivering in the darkness.

Brick boy, reached into his pocket and felt his trusty pocket lighter and reassured everyone.

"It will be ok everyone. I will relight everyone's candle with my family's pocket lighter we use to keep our fireplace going."

They were resilient and they relit their flames.

"We need to build protection from the big bad wind!" the candles said in unison.

As they relit their flames,
the big bad wind retreated,
defeated.

The candles knew they needed protection.

"We really need protection from that big bad wind", they all agreed.

"I know! Let's build sconces to protect our candles!" they decided.

"We could build sconces to protect us out here, kind of like a house protects people, the sconces will protect us" suggested brick boy.

So, instead of building houses like the people do for protection, they decided to craft sconces.

Each sconce was unique:

"I will build my sconce out of wax" said the littlest princess candle.

So, the first candle, the littlest princess, built her sconce out of wax.

It was delicate, its glow warm and inviting, just like she is.

Glistening metal candle boy, the second candle, chose glass for his sconce.

His sconce sparkled and glistened reflecting the moonlight just like he did.

Brick boy, the third candle, was wise and practical.

He built his sconce out of sturdy bricks.

The little candles were so very proud of their hard work and the sconces they had built for protection.

Each sconce a unique and beautiful reflection of the hard work and the personality of the person who had made it.

All too soon, the big bad wind returned, relentless as ever.

The big bad wind came in howling and blowing harder than ever this time.

The big bad wind blew against the wax sconce, melting it away.

The big bad wind blew against the glass sconce and shattered it into a thousand pieces.

But when the big bad wind blew against the brick sconce, it stood firm, unyielding.

The big bad wind huffed and puffed, trying once more but it couldn't break the brick sconce.

Defeated, the big bad wind finally gave up and vanished into the night.

And so, the three little candles seeing the wisdom of brick sconces, decided they should all have them.

The littlest princess candle had hers made of bricks to look like she was living in her very own castle!

So ever though her sconces was made of bricks, it was still very unique like she is.

Glistening metal candle boy, the second candle, added a touch of metal, of course, to his brick sconce.

His unique glistening metal body glistened even more in his new shiny brick and metal sconce!

And of course, brick boys, sconce remained brick.

Why change a good thing when its working for you!

The three little candles teach us that you don't have to lose your individuality to be safe and do what is right to keep the rest of the world safe too.

You just have to be open to the options around you.

They lived happily ever after, their flames flickering brightly within their protective brick sconces.

They learned that strength lies not only in fire but also in resilience and clever choices.

"We are the candle-brick trio, unbreakable and forever aglow."

And whenever the wind howled, they would whisper to each other:

"We are the candle-brick trio, unbreakable and forever aglow."

The End.

About the Authors
Cade Brand

Cade Brand is a remarkable and imaginative young author at the tender age of six. With a zest for life, Cade embraces adventures at the beach, in the park, and even in the magical worlds of Iron Man and Mickey Mouse. His creative spirit shines through as he weaves delightful tales alongside his beloved sister Aurora, his doting Mommy Tamara, his wise Papaw John, and his loving Mamaw Lady Kimberly.

Now, Cade is ready to embark on a new chapter in his young life as he proudly presents his very first full-length story to the world. With boundless enthusiasm and a twinkle in his eye, Cade invites readers of all ages to join him on this heartwarming literary journey filled with inspiration, laughter, and joy. Get ready to be captivated by the imagination of a young author, as Cade's words transport you to extraordinary places where dreams come true and anything is possible.

Lady Kimberly Motes Doty

Lady Kimberly Motes Doty is a remarkable woman who has devoted her life to making a positive impact on others. As a minister, she selflessly guides individuals in discovering their spiritual path, offering them solace and support along their journey. Her role as a life coach allows her to empower others to live their lives to the fullest, providing guidance and encouragement every step of the way.

Lady Kimberly's expertise extends beyond the realm of spiritual and emotional well-being. As a natural health specialist, she possesses a wealth of knowledge on maintaining optimal physical health and wellness. Her dedication to holistic living inspires others to prioritize self-care and embrace a healthy lifestyle.

In addition to her various roles in helping and guiding others, Lady Kimberly is also a talented writer and sage. Through her writings, she shares her wisdom and insights, providing inspiration and guidance to those who seek it. Her words have the power to uplift and enlighten, leaving a lasting impact on those who read them.

When Lady Kimberly isn't immersed in her work, she finds immense joy in spending quality time with her cherished family. Whether it's creating precious memories with her beloved grandson Cade or simply enjoying the company of her loved ones, family holds a special place in Lady Kimberly's heart.

Lady Kimberly Motes Doty's unwavering dedication to helping others, her passion for writing, and her love for family make her an extraordinary grandmother, editor, and publisher for Cade. With her guidance and support, Cade's exceptional talent as a young author is sure to shine brightly for the world to see.

https://ladykimberlyindustries.com

https://mybook.to/LadyKimberlyBooks

More about Cade & Lady Kimberly

The moment Cade, my precious grandson, approached me with his desire to write a story, my heart overflowed with joy and excitement. Despite his tender age in kindergarten, I couldn't help but wonder what he would be able to contribute. However, to my utter delight, Cade surprised me beyond measure.

With an unwavering determination, Cade had not just a mere story idea, but an entire narrative meticulously crafted in his young imagination. His eyes sparkled with enthusiasm as he turned to me and said, "Mamaw, can you type this for me?" In that moment, I knew something extraordinary was about to unfold.

Swiftly, my fingers danced across the keyboard, eagerly capturing every word Cade shared. I had anticipated a simple outline, but to my astonishment, Cade had intricately woven together a complete storyline. Together, we transformed his imaginative musings into beautifully crafted sentences, ensuring his narrative came to life.

As a grandmother, my heart swells with indescribable pride. Cade's remarkable accomplishment at such a tender age is a testament to his creativity, passion, and innate storytelling ability. Congratulations, Cade, on your first captivating story. Your determination and talent have ignited a flame within my heart, inspiring me and countless others to pursue our own dreams fearlessly!

Enchanted Seashell
A Magical Beach Adventure
Lady Kimberly Motes Doty

Conor's Magical Treasure Hunt
Get ready for an enchanting adventure with Conor and his wise grandmother, Mimi, in this inspiring tale of love, discovery, and the magic of the sea. Join them as they set off on a treasure hunt to find the perfect Conch shell, rumored to possess a magical sound.
Lady Kimberly Motes Doty

Treasure Hunters
A Beachcombing Adventure
Lady Kimberly Motes Doty

"If the Alphabet Grew Out of The Sea" V1 - in English, French & Spanish

"If The Alphabet Grew Out of The Sea v2" - Almost 600 pages of mazes, word searches and fun facts about sea animals on an exciting Sea Adventure!

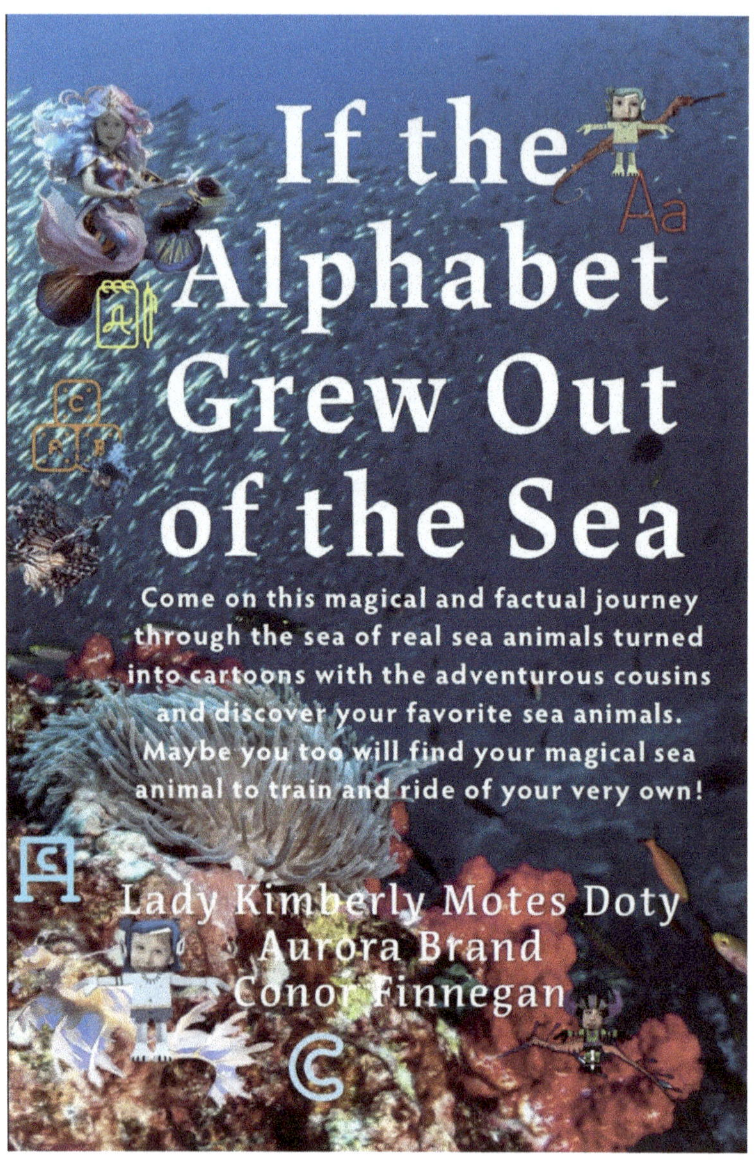

A children's book series written by children for children!

"The Whimsical World of the Three Littles: 125+ Silly Variations That Will Make You Squeal with Laughter"

Welcome to "The Whimsical World of the Littles, a 125+ Silly Variations That Will Make You Squeal with Laughter"! Get ready to embark on a delightful journey through the enchanting tales like you've never experienced before. This extraordinary collection brings together over 125 whimsical and hilarious variations of the classic story, guaranteed to tickle your funny bone and ignite your imagination.

In this imaginative world, the littles take on new adventures, encounter peculiar characters, and face unexpected challenges in the most playful and entertaining ways. From pirates sailing the bacon seas to astronauts exploring the hamisphere, each story will transport you to a world filled with laughter, surprises, and endless joy.

Join the mischievous trio as they build their houses with unconventional materials like pillows, marshmallows, bubblegum, and even cotton candy.

Encounter wacky versions of the big bad wolf, who might just turn out to be a big bad wall, a goofball or a big bad hipster with a penchant for organic kale.

These imaginative twists and turns will keep you giggling and guessing until the very end.

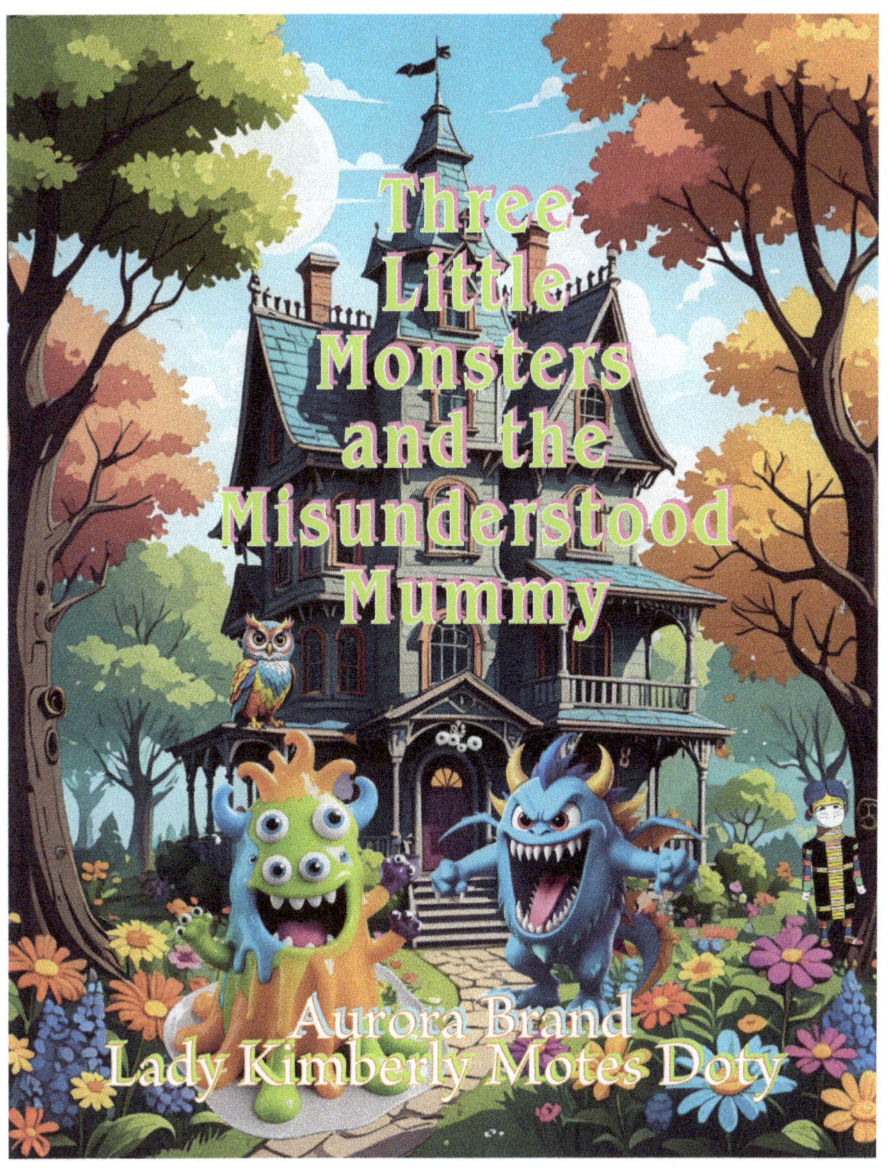

Three Little Monsters and the Misunderstood Mummy
Aurora Brand
Lady Kimberly Motes Doty

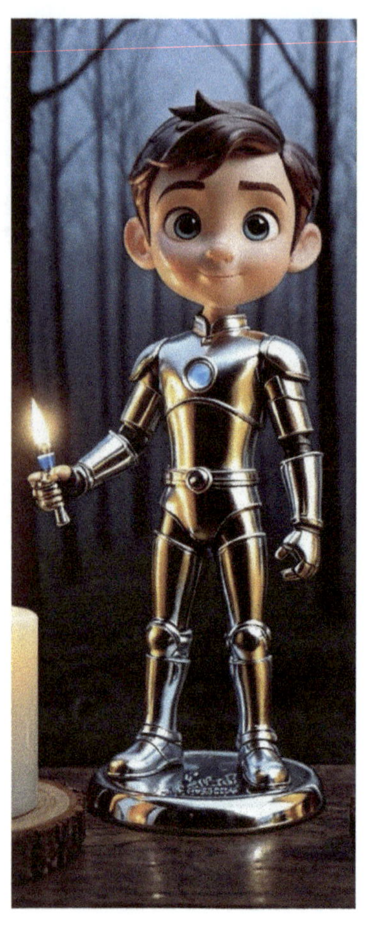

Hey, we forgot to ask you,
what would your brick
sconce look like?

Yes, each time you come to visit and read about us, you can imagine you are in your own brick sconce with us.

Would your brick sconce look like a castle like mine, or have shiny metal or what would you do to your brick sconce to make it unique for you?

We can't wait to find out!

Imagine your very own brick sconce here in forest candle village with us and draw or write a description of it.